STAY CONNECTED

All Social Media Links

www.chefmorley.com

Letter from the editor:

I have had the honor of collaborating with Erin since 2020. To say that she is one of the most genuine, down-to-earth and generous people is an understatement. I don't know where I would be without her. She always has nothing but the best intentions in mind and always strives to put forth recipes that not only taste good, but that fit into a low carb living. Whether you are keto, low-carb or just trying to eat a balanced diet.

I truly hope you enjoy our creation of this 3rd e-book. She put a lot of love and thought into each and every one of her recipes, and I did the same with bringing them to life. Each recipe contains links to the TikTok video of her making the recipe or the link to her Instagram post with the recipe. Just open up the camera on your smart phone and point at the code. It will bring up a link for you to click and will take you to the recipe.

We tried to make it easy for you to find some of the ingredients she uses that may not be easily accessible in stores. You will find a little 🛒 by each item that she has linked in her "amazon must haves". Please keep in mind that Amazon's stock and prices fluctuate and may have changed since the items were listed in this e-book. You may be able to find it at a better price in store, but we listed them for your convenience of ordering on-line.

Thank you all for your continued support of our amazing Chef Erin Morley.
And to Erin, thank you for being authentic, thank you for being you. I look forward to working with you for many, many years to come.

Sarah J Dunnuck

Appetizers & Light Fairs

 - Vegetarian   - Mild   - Spicy

Dips, Dressings & Sauces

**Kitchen Food Hack: Are you having trouble peeling your hardboiled eggs? Add 1 tsp baking soda per liter of water when boiling them and the shells should just peel right off.

Ⓥ - Vegetarian   🌶 - Mild   🌶 - Spicy

Sides

Breakfast Hack: Take a screw top container (yes, it has to be screw top). Scramble a couple of eggs in there. Add sausage and cheese or whatever you want. Put the top back on, put in the fridge for an easy grab and go to throw in the microwave later.

(V) - Vegetarian   🌶 - Mild   🌶 - Spicy

Mains

 - Vegetarian   - Mild   - Spicy

Mains

Chef's Tip: Have a stainless steel pan you don't like to use because stuff always sticks to it? Put pan on stove top with nothing in it. Turn heat on high and get it piping hot. Add cold healthy fat oil to piping hot pan. It will automatically shimmer. Turn heat down then immediately add protein. Don't touch it until its ready to flip. It should flip without sticking

Ⓥ - Vegetarian　　　　 - Mild　　　　 - Spicy

Treats

Appetizers
&
Light Fairs

Potato Chips

Macros per ½ cp cooked: 3 net carb | 12g fat | 1g protein | 21 cal

[3/21 Video]

Ingredients:

Celery Root

Kosher Salt

Olive Oil Cooking Spray

Directions:

Preheat oven to 400 ºF

Peel the celery root

Using a mandolin or sharp knife, slice celery root into thin slices

Sprinkle with salt and let sit for 15 minutes while all water draws out then pat completely dry

Lay in a single layer on a parchment lined baking sheet and bake for 18- 25 minutes

Fried Pickles

Macros per 4-5 pickles:: 2 net carb | 10g fat | 6g protein | 109 cal   [3/19 Video]

Ingredients:

Dill pickle slices   1 egg

1 cp Keto and Co Flatbread & Pizza Mix 🛒   3 Tsp avocado oil

Directions:

Dry pickles as much as possible

Dip in egg then dip in keto and co flatbread & pizza mix

With a little avocado oil in a non-stick skillet, brown pickles on both sides

Fried Goat Cheese Balls w/sugar free honey

Yields: 12 servings   Macros per serving: 1.2 net carb | 5.3g fat | 6.2g protein | 84 cal

[1/12 Video]

Ingredients:

8oz goat cheese	½ cp nutritional yeast 🛒	sugar free honey 🛒
¼ cp pea protein 🛒	½ cp almond flour 🛒	1 ½ cps grapeseed oil
2 beaten eggs	pepper to taste	

Directions:

To one bowl add pea protein

To a second bowl add 2 beaten eggs

To a 3rd bowl add nutritional yeast, almond flour and pepper

Roll goat cheese into equal size balls

Dip each ball into pea protein, then into the egg, then into the nutritional yeast mixture

Put in freezer for 1 hour

Add oil with a high smoke point to a small saucepan (healthy fat oil only)

Heat to around 370ºF

Fry for about 30 seconds each

Carefully remove and then drizzle with sugar free honey

Crispy Ranch Chicken Wings

Yields: 6 servings   Macros per serving: .5 net carb | 25g fat | 36g protein | 385 cal   [1/9 Video]

Ingredients:

2 lbs chicken wings

1 Tbsp baking powder

1 Tbsp Flavor God Ranch 🛒

Salt to taste

Directions:

Preheat oven to 425 °F

Pat wings as dry as you can get them

Put wings in a large bowl

Add salt, baking powder and Flavor God Ranch seasoning and mix together

Put in a single layer on a parchment lined baking sheet

Bake for 25 minutes, flip and then bake for another 20 minutes

Dip in homemade ranch, optional (recipe here)

Thai Chili Chicken Wings

Yields: 6 servings Macros per serving: 1.6 net carb | 25g fat | 36g protein | 388 cal   [1/26 Video]

Ingredients:

2 lbs chicken wings

1 Tbsp baking powder

Salt

Pepper

Sweet Thai Chili Sauce:

⅓ cp water

⅓ cp allulose 🛒

2 cloves garlic

2 tsp red pepper flakes or diced whole Thai chilis

pinch salt

xanthan gum 🛒

Directions:

Preheat oven to 425 °F

Pat wings as dry as you can get them

Put wings in a large bowl

Add salt, baking powder and mix together

Put in a single layer on a parchment lined baking sheet

Bake for 25 minutes, flip and then bake for another 20 minutes

While wings are baking, make your Thai Chili Sauce

In a small saucepan add ⅓ cp water

Dice Thai chili peppers (these are super spicy, if you want it less spicy use red pepper flakes instead)

To saucepan add allulose and garlic clove

Whisk until allulose is dissolved

Add chili peppers (or red pepper flakes) and xanthan gum whisk until thick

Put in fridge to cool

When wings are cooked and crispy toss in Thai chili sauce

Chicken Tenders

Yields: 6 servings   Macros per 2-3 tenders: 3 net carb | 19g fat | 38g protein | 211 cal   [1/24 Video]

Ingredients:

2 lbs chicken tenders

1 ½ cps keto flour 🛒

½ cp grated parmesan

Salt & Pepper to taste

Flavor God Everything Spicy (or seasoning of choice) 🛒

1 cp avocado oil

2 beaten eggs

Directions:

Beat eggs in 1 bowl

To another bowl add flour, parmesan, salt & pepper and seasoning of choice

Add healthy oil to a non-stick skillet and fry chicken for 5-7 minutes on each side, depending on thickness

BBQ Chicken Lollipops

Yields: 5 servings   Macros per serving: .5 net carb | 25g fat | 49g protein | 336cal   (1/14 Video)

Ingredients:

2 lbs drumsticks

Flavor God Honey BBQ 🛒

1 cp sugar-free BBQ sauce

3 Tbsp butter

Directions:

Preheat oven to 400 ºF

Pat drumsticks dry

Carefully using a really sharp knife cut off the end by the meat so they stand up straight

Score the bone at the other end and pull down the meat towards the bottom

Using a paper towel pull off the excess skin

Wrap each of the bones in foil

Liberally season with whatever seasoning you like, I am using Flavor God Honey BBQ

Bake for 30 minutes

In a saucepan heat sugar free BBQ sauce and butter

Once melted dip each drumstick in to coat and put back on tray and bake for another 15 minutes

Boneless Buffalo Wings

Yields: 4 servings   Macros per serving: 2 net carb | 35g fat | 46g protein | 402 cal   [3/16 Video]

Ingredients:

1 lb chicken tenders	2 tsp garlic powder
2 eggs	1 tsp onion powder
1 cp almond flour 🛒	1 cp Franks buffalo sauce
1 cp parmesan cheese	1 cp avocado oil

Directions:

In a large bowl scramble the eggs and then add the chicken tenders

In another bowl add your dry ingredients

Take each chicken tender and let the excess egg drip off then dredge into the mixture

In small saucepan add your buffalo sauce of choice and heat on low

Cook chicken tenders in a healthy oil such as avocado oil in a non-stick skillet

When cooked through toss in a large bowl with warmed buffalo sauce

Pair with carrots, celery sticks and homemade blue cheese dressing (recipe)

Hash Browns

Yields: 6 servings   Macros per 1 hash brown: 1.3 net carb | 33g fat | 2.3g protein | 44 cal   [3/30 Video]

Ingredients:

1 small cauliflower

¼ cp sour cream

   or shredded cheese

1 tsp baking powder

½ tsp paprika

¼ tsp onion powder

2 Tbsp almond flour 🛒

1 egg

Kosher salt to taste

pepper to taste

Directions:

Preheat oven to 400 °F

Remove stem and leaves from cauliflower then put the cauliflower in a food processor until it is nice and fine

Put in in microwave safe dish and microwave for 3 minutes in high

Drop mixture on clean kitchen towel or cheesecloth and wring out as much liquid as you can

In a mixing bowl add cauliflower and remaining ingredients

Drop onto parchment lined baking sheet in whatever shape you want

Bake for 30 minutes

California Chicken Sandwich

Macros per sandwich: 5 net carb | 33g fat | 24.6g protein | 438 cal

[K3 Video]

Ingredients:

Fresh spinach

Sliced tomato

Boneless skinless chicken breasts

2 Tbsp avocado oil

Garlic salt

Pepper

Bacon bun

Bacon

Guacamole

3 ripe avocados

½ cp red onion

1 Tbsp lemon juice

⅓ cp fresh cilantro

1 jalapeño

½ tsp kosher salt

6 cherry tomatoes

Directions:

Refer to bacon bun video and guacamole video

Take your tempered chicken and season all sides

In a non-stick skillet with avocado oil, fry chicken on both sides until cooked through

Put chicken, homemade guacamole, spinach and tomato between bacon buns

Cabbage Roll in a Bowl

Yields: 10 servings   Macros per serving: 5.1 net carb | 5g fat | 14g protein | 131 cal

[1/4 Video]

Ingredients:

1 small white onion	3 cloves minced garlic	1 lb grass-fed beef
2 Tbsp olive oil	½ cp low sodium beef broth	1 tsp smoked paprika
2 cp cauliflower rice	2 Tbsp tomato paste	1 tsp onion powder
1 small head cabbage	1 can diced tomatoes	Salt & Pepper

Directions:

Add olive oil to dutch oven or a large pot

Dice onion and add to the pot and cook until translucent

Add cauliflower rice

Add garlic and cook for 30 seconds, until fragment

Add low sodium beef broth and tomato paste and cook down

Add beef and remaining spices

Cook on high until all juices evaporate

Add diced tomatoes and cook down until liquid evaporates

Cut cabbage into bite size pieces and throw on top

Cover and cook for 20 minutes until cabbage is tender

Jalapeño Popper Chicken Salad

Yields: 6 servings   Macros per serving (chicken salad only): 2.8 net carb | 19g fat | 26g protein | 302 cal   [1/6 Insta]

Ingredients:

2 cups cooked shredded chicken

2/3 cup Mayo made with olive oil

3 oz room temp cream cheese

1/4 cup finely chopped jalapeño

1/4 cup finely chopped red onion

5 sliced cook crumbled bacon (optional)

1/2 cup shredded sharp cheddar (optional)

Salt and pepper to taste

Directions:

Mix all ingredients together and serve on a Wasa cracker (macros are for chicken salad only)

For a healthier option, leave out bacon and cheese

Asian Slaw Turkey Wraps

Yields: 10 servings   Macros per serving: 2.1 net carb | 9.5g fat | 15g protein | 157 cal   [2/19 Video]

Ingredients:

Marinade:

1 Tbsp liquid aminos

3 Tbsp toasted sesame oil

1 Tbsp mirin

1 Tbsp water

3 Tbsp erythritol

Slaw:

1 ½ cp napa cabbage

1 small carrot-julienned

1 small red pepper-julienned

1 small cucumber-julienned

2 green onions

Filling:

1 lb ground turkey

½ tsp ginger

1 clove garlic-minced

2 Tbsp natural peanut butter

2 Tbsp liquid aminos

1 Tbsp toasted sesame oil

Sesame seeds

Red pepper flakes

Butter lettuce (for wraps)

Directions:

Add all marinade ingredients to a small bowl, whisk together until sweetener is dissolved

Chop all veggies and add to a large bowl and toss with marinade, cover and put in fridge while you make your filling

In a non-stick skillet cook ground turkey until cooked through, then put on high and cook until all liquid evaporates

Add all remaining filling ingredients

Add marinated slaw and ground turkey to butter lettuce and enjoy!

Fried Okra Chaffle

Yields: 2 chaffles   Macros per chaffle: 2.5 net carb | 11g fat | 6g protein | 138 cal   [3/29 Video]

Ingredients:

1 egg	3 Tbsp almond flour 🛒
1 ½ Tbsp sour cream	salt & pepper to taste
1 tsp Tony's	2 Tbsp mozzarella cheese-divided
¼ tsp onion powder	
2 pieces okra-sliced	

Directions:

Pre-heat mini waffle maker

Mix all ingredients (except cheese)

Sprinkle ½ Tbsp cheese on the bottom of the mini waffle maker

Pour ½ of mixed ingredients

Sprinkle ½ Tbsp cheese on top

Close lid and cook for approx. 2 minutes or until crisp

Repeat with 2nd chaffle

Seaweed Snack

Macros per serving: 2 net carb | 15g fat | 4g protein | 173 cal

[3/25 Video]

Ingredients:

Piece of seaweed

Almond milk cream cheese (or regular is fine too)

Avocado

Sriracha

Everything But the Bagel Seasoning or sesame seeds

Directions:

Put a little cream cheese on ½ the seaweed

Put a couple slices of avocado

Top with sriracha and seasoning

Fold over and enjoy!

Roasted Caprese Tomatoes

Macros per tomato: 5 net carb | 19g fat | 10g protein | 280 cal

[3/31 Video]

Ingredients:

½ cp balsamic vinegar

1 Tbsp brown sugar swerve 🛒

Tomatoes

Kosher salt

pepper

Fresh mozzarella

Fresh basil

Drizzle olive oil

Directions:

Preheat oven to 375 °F

In a small saucepan add balsamic vinegar and brown sugar swerve

Keep stirring until all it reduces by half and turns into a glaze

Slice tomatoes in half

Liberally season with salt and pepper

Put mozzarella on bottom of each half and top with basil

Put tops of tomatoes back on

Drizzle with olive oil, sprinkle with kosher salt and pop in the oven for 20 minutes

Drizzle with balsamic glaze before serving

Chicken Nuggets

Yields: 6 servings   Macros per serving: 4.8 net carb | 19g fat | 22g protein | 274 cal

[3/1 Video]

Ingredients:

1 lb ground chicken

1 cp mozzarella

1 tsp Old Bay

1 tsp garlic salt

pepper to taste

¼ cp vital wheat gluten

2 beaten eggs

1 cp almond flour

½ cp nutritional yeast flakes

Avocado oil

Directions:

In a bowl combine ground chicken, mozzarella, old bay, garlic salt and pepper

Mix with hands

Make nugget shapes and put in freezer 1 hr

Create an assembly line

In 1 bowl put wheat gluten (omit if gluten intolerant)

In a 2nd bowl put eggs

In a 3rd bowl mix flour and yeast flakes

Dredge each nugget in the following order:

Gluten, eggs, flour/yeast

Fry in avocado oil until internal temp is 175°F

Dips

Dressings

&

Sauces

Mini Sweet Pepper Feta Dip

Macros per ¼ cp: 4 net carb | 20g fat | 9g protein | 220 cal

[3/18 Video]

Ingredients:

1 lb block feta	Red pepper flakes
½ lb mini sweet peppers	Drizzle Olive oil
½ bulb garlic	⅓ cp mozzarella
Kosher salt	Fresh basil-garnish
Pepper	

Directions:

Preheat oven to 375 ºF

Put feta cheese in casserole dish

Add sweet mini peppers, ½ bulb of garlic, red chili flakes, kosher salt and pepper and drizzle with olive oil

Bake 30-35 min

Pop garlic out of the bulb and give it a good mix and chop the peppers into bite size pieces

Top with mozzarella cheese and basil

Buffalo Chicken Dip

Yields: 6 servings   Macros per serving: 1.5 net carb | 17g fat | 13g protein | 214 cal   [2/12 Video]

Ingredients:

2 lbs boneless skinless chicken breasts-cooked/shredded

¼ - ½ cp low sodium chicken broth

4 oz room temp cream cheese

¼ cp sour cream

¼ cp avocado mayo

½ cp Frank's red hot sauce

pepper to taste

Directions:

In a large bowl, shred cooked chicken breasts with a hand mixer

As you are mixing, add low sodium chicken broth until meat starts to come together

Mix in rest of ingredients

(When choosing a mayo, please choose one with avocado oil, its better for you)

Put in fridge for a couple hours

Chef tip: You can even use this to stuff into jalapeno peppers to make poppers

Caesar Salad Dressing

Macros per 2 Tbps: .5 net carb | 17g fat | 3.1g protein | 160 cal   [3/12 Video]

Ingredients:

1 cp avocado mayo	1 tsp Worcestershire
2 cloves minced garlic	1 tsp anchovy paste
4 Tbsp fresh lemon juice	½ cp finely shredded parmesan
1 tsp dijon	salt & pepper to taste

Directions:

Put everything together in a small mason jar

Give it a good shake and put in fridge

**Keeps for up to 2 weeks

I added mine to dressing containers  I found on Amazon

Feta Vinaigrette

Macros per 2 Tbsp: .7 net carb | 10g fat | 2.6g protein | 104 cal   [2/17 Video]

Ingredients:

8 oz feta cheese	2 tsp oregano
4 Tbsp water	salt & pepper to taste
6 Tbsp red wine vinegar	up to $\frac{1}{3}$ cp extra virgin olive oil

Directions:

Add all ingredients except for olive oil to a food processor or high power blender

Blend together then slowly stream in extra virgin olive oil until you get a nice, creamy, smooth consistency

I added mine to dressing containers 🛒 I found on Amazon

Greek Dressing

Yields: 10 servings Macros per serving: 1.3 net carb | 22g fat | .4g protein | 202 cal

[1/16 Insta]

Ingredients:

½ cp fresh lemon juice

¼ cp red wine vinegar

1 cp olive oil

2 Tbsp grated parmesan

1 tsp thyme

3 cloves minced garlic

salt & pepper to taste

Directions:

Mix all ingredients together and refrigerated for at least 2 hours before using

I added mine to dressing containers 🛒 I found on Amazon

Sauce

Macros (for sauce only) per cup: 4 net carb | 6g fat | 1.2g protein | 97 cal   [2/24 Video]

Ingredients:

½ cp olive oil	1 cp red wine	Fresh basil
½ cp onion	1 large can san Marzano peeled tomatoes	Rind of parmesan cheese
Red pepper flakes	1 large can crushed tomatoes	Kosher salt
Italian sausage	3 Tbsp tomato paste	Homemade meatballs (recipe)
6 cloves sliced garlic	1 tsp sugar	

Directions:

To a large pot add olive oil, diced onion, kosher salt and red pepper flakes

Put Italian sausages in the pot and brown them all on sides, take out and set aside

When onions become translucent add garlic and cook until fragrant, about 30 seconds

Deglaze pot with red wine

Cook the red wine until it reduces by half then add tomatoes and tomato paste

Add in more kosher salt and 1 tsp sugar to cut the acidity

Using a potato masher, mash all ingredients together

If you have a rind of parmesan cheese, add that to the pot with a whole stem of fresh basil

Add Italian sausages and meatballs in the pot, cover and simmer for 1 hr (at least)

Remove the rind before enjoying

Ranch Dressing

Macros 2 Tbsp: .3 net carb | 1.9g fat | 2.6g protein | 147 cal   [3/5 Video]

Ingredients:

½ cp avocado mayo   1 tsp onion powder

½ cp sour cream   1 tsp garlic powder

¼ cp heavy cream   2/3 tsp fresh lemon

1 tsp dill

Directions:

Mix all ingredients together and refrigerated for at least 2 hours before using

I added mine to dressing containers 🛒 I found on Amazon

Pico de Gallo

Yields: 10 servings   Macros per serving: 2.9 net carb | .2g fat | .7g protein | 17 cal   [3/5 Video]

Ingredients:

½ cp white onion   1 jalapeño pepper-seeded

Kosher salt to taste   5-6 plum tomatoes

¼ cp fresh lime juice   ½ cp chopped cilantro

Directions:

Dice up the onion and jalapeño and add to a bowl with kosher salt and lime juice (add more jalapeño peppers if you like it spicy)

Mix together and set aside

Chop the tomatoes and add to the bowl

Mix in chopped cilantro

Taste as you go and add more kosher salt to your liking

Cover and refrigerate for 24 hours

Drain before use

Sides

Warm Brussels Slaw

Yields: 6 servings   Macros per serving: 3 net carb | 7g fat | 2.8g protein | 90 cal   [3/26 Video]

Ingredients:

1 lb brussels sprouts   pepper to taste

4 slices cooked bacon   1 Tbsp sugar free honey

½ shallot or red onion   3 Tbsp balsamic vinegar

⅓ cp slivered almonds   4 Tbsp olive oil

Directions:

Cut off the bottoms of the brussels sprouts and carefully cut them into shredded pieces

Cook bacon in a skillet, remove, crumble and set aside, reserve the bacon grease

To the reserved grease add slivered almonds and thinly sliced shallots

Once translucent add in brussels sprouts and crumbled bacon and season with pepper

In a small bowl whisk together sugar free honey, balsamic vinegar and olive oil

Add to pan and toss until warmed through

Cold Greek Cauliflower Salad

Macros per ½ cp: 2.8 net carb | 15g fat | 4.6g protein | 169 cal   [1/16 Video]

Ingredients:

½ small head purple cauliflower   ¼ cp fresh parsley

½ small head white cauliflower   ½ cp feta cheese

1 small red onion diced   salt & pepper to taste

½ cp kalamata olives

Directions:

Chop cauliflower into tiny bit sized pieces and add to a mixing bowl

Chop red onion and olives nice and small and add to mixing bowl

Add feta cheese, parsley, salt & pepper and mix to combine

Mix in homemade Greek dressing (recipe)

Cover and put in fridge for 2 hours before enjoying

Asian Style Cucumber Salad

Yields: 5 servings   Macros per serving: 4.1 net carb | .8g fat | 2.3g protein | 37 cal   [1/20 Video]

Ingredients:

6 mini cucumbers

Sauce:

2 Tbsp liquid aminos

2 cloves garlic minced

3 tsp brown sugar swerve 🛒

½ Tbsp toasted sesame oil

1 Tbsp rice wine vinegar

salt & pepper

red pepper flakes to taste

Directions:

Chop ends of mini cucumbers and with the flat end of a large knife carefully smash down and roughly chop it

Add to a bowl and liberally season with kosher salt (this helps draw out the moisture)

Let sit in fridge for 20 minutes

In a small mixing bowl whisk all of the ingredients for the sauce

Take the cucumbers out of the fridge and drain out liquid

Add the sauce to the cucumbers and toss to mix

Add more kosher salt and red pepper flakes to taste

Let sit in fridge for 2 hours before enjoying

Roasted Broccoli

Yields: 8 servings   Macros per serving: 3.3 net carb | 4g fat | 3g protein | 66 cal   [1/21 Video]

Ingredients:

Broccoli

Olive oil

Salt & Pepper

Garlic Lovers-Flavor God 🛒

parmigiano-reggiano

½ Lemon

Directions:

Preheat oven to 400 °F

On a parchment lined baking sheet put equal size broccoli florets and drizzle with olive oil

Season with salt & pepper and seasoning of choice, I am using Garlic Lovers from Flavor God

Squeeze the juice of ½ lemon on top

Roast for 25 minutes

Shave fresh parmigiano-reggiano on top before serving

Roasted Brussels Sprouts w/Crispy Pancetta & Hazelnuts

Yields: 6 servings   Macros per serving: 4 net carb | 20g fat | 8g protein | 239 cal   [1/30 Video]

Ingredients:

1 lb brussels sprouts	zest 1 lemon
1 Tbsp olive oil	juice 1 lemon
1 ¼ cp pancetta	Pepper to taste
1 cp chopped hazelnuts	flake salt to taste 🛒

Directions:

Cut off the ends of the brussels sprouts then cut them in half and put them in a large pot

Heavily season with kosher salt and boil for 2 minutes, drain and set aside

Finely chop up hazelnuts and chop pancetta into small pieces

In a large skillet brown pancetta in olive oil

Once it starts to get crispy and add in hazelnuts to toast

Toss brussels sprouts into skillet

Cook on medium high until they start to brown

Season with pepper

Toss in zest of 1 lemon and juice of 1 lemon

Once hot add to a bowl and top with flake salt

Roasted Curry Green Beans

Yields: 4 servings   Macros per serving: 3.5 net carb | 14g fat | 1.7g protein | 150 cal

[2/4 Video]

Ingredients:

12 oz bag green beans

1 Tbsp curry powder

Kosher salt

pepper

drizzle olive oil

flake salt to taste 🛒

Directions:

Preheat oven to 400 °F

In a large bowl add green beans, curry powder, kosher salt, pepper and olive oil and toss together

Put directly on a baking sheet in a single layer

Bake for 20 minutes, take them out and toss them around and then bake for another 10 minutes

Top with flake salt

Salt n Vinegar Cauliflower

Yields: 4 servings   Macros per serving: 5 net carb | 28g fat | 5g protein | 301 cal

[3/10 Video]

Ingredients:

1 small cauliflower	2 tsp dill
¼ cp olive oil	kosher salt to taste
2-3 Tbsp white vinegar	chopped chives (optional)

Directions:

Preheat oven to 450 ºF with your baking pan in there while it preheats

Cut cauliflower into bit size florets

In a small bowl whisk together vinegar and dill

Carefully remove pre-heated pan from oven and drizzle with olive oil

Put cauliflower into pan

Drizzle with olive oil and sprinkle on kosher salt

Bake for 15 minutes, toss then broil on high until crisp

Take out of oven and stir and then mix in vinegar and dill mixture

Top with chives (optional)

Lemon Pepper Brussels Sprouts

Yields: 6 servings   Macros per serving: 4 net carb | 9g fat | 2.6g protein | 113 cal   [2/25 Video]

Ingredients:

1 lb brussels sprouts

¼ cp olive oil

1 lemon zest and juice

Coarse ground pepper to taste

kosher salt to taste

2 cloves minced garlic

2 Tbsp fresh chives (optional)

1-2 Tbsp chopped lemongrass (optional)

Directions:

To a small saucepan add olive oil and long strips of lemon zest and turn heat to medium

Cut ends off brussels sprouts then slice in half and put on a baking sheet

When lemon zest starts to sizzle take off heat and drizzle the oil over the brussels sprouts

Season with salt and pepper

*Optional: finely chop lemongrass and sprinkle on top

Cook under broiler 12-15 minutes, tossing halfway through

Chop up fresh chives and sprinkle over top and squeeze juice of lemon over brussels sprouts

Zucchini Stacks

Yields: 12 servings   Macros per serving: .5 net carb | 3.8g fat | 2.3g protein | 50 cal   [2/9 Video]

Ingredients:

1 medium zucchini	1 tsp everything but elote (or seasoning of choice)
¼ cp oat fiber	1 cp fresh grated pecorino romano
½ cp almond flour	2 eggs. beaten
Salt & pepper	

Directions:

Preheat oven to 400 °F

To a small bowl oat fiber, almond flour, seasonings, salt and pepper (I'm using Everything But Elote)

In another bowl beat 2 eggs

In a 3rd bowl grate fresh pecorino romano or use grated parmesan

Using a mandolin or sharp knife and thinly slice zucchini

Dip each slice into the beaten egg

Then dip into pecorino romano or parmesan

Stack the slices, when it gets to be 5-6 tall, take the stack and dip into dry mixture and put on a parchment lined baking sheet

Top with a little more shredded romano or parmesan, salt & pepper

Bake for 15 minutes

Caramelized Balsamic Zucchini

Macros per 1 small zucchini: 4.7 net carb | 11g fat | 4g protein | 137 cal   [2/6 Video]

Ingredients:

3 small zucchini	¼ cp balsamic vinegar
½ cp cherry tomatoes	1 Tbsp butter
Crumbled feta to taste	avocado oil

Directions:

Preheat oven to 400 ºF

Heat cast iron skillet

Cut ends off of zucchini then slice in half the long way

Using a paring knife score zucchini flesh diagonally one way then score the opposite way making little x's

Using a paper towel get the zucchini as dry as you can

Sprinkle with kosher salt then put face side down in a hot cast iron skillet with avocado oil

Once caramelized flip over

Turn of heat and add butter, balsamic vinegar, tomatoes, salt & pepper

Carefully put pan in oven and bake for 15 minutes

Top with feta cheese (optional)

Asparagus with Dijon Sauce

Yields: 4 servings   Macros per serving: 3 net carb | 7.5g fat | .7g protein | 97 cal   [2/10 Video]

Ingredients:

1-2 bunches asparagus

Extra virgin olive oil

Salt & pepper to taste

¼ cp low sodium chicken broth

1 clove minced garlic

3 Tbsp Dijon mustard

juice 1 lemon

zest ½ lemon

1 tsp dill

Directions:

Preheat oven to 425 ºF

Take 1 asparagus spear and give a snap towards the end

Wherever it naturally breaks, you know you can cut off the ends of the other spears

Lay in a single layer on a parchment lined baking sheet and drizzle with olive oil, salt & pepper

Bake for 10-15 minutes

While the asparagus is baking, take a small saucepan and add remaining ingredients

Cook on medium-high, bring to a boil and then lower heat and cook until it reduces by half until it thickens

Pour over asparagus before serving

Roasted Turmeric Cauliflower w/crispy shallots

Yields: 4 servings   Macros per serving: 2.5 net carb | 13g fat | 1.5g protein | 141 cal   [1/5 Video]

Ingredients:

1 small head cauliflower   ¼ cp olive oil

1 large shallot   1 Tbsp turmeric

Salt & pepper

Directions:

Preheat oven to 425 ºF

To a bowl add thinly slice shallot

Cut off leaves and stem from cauliflower and cut into equal bite size florets and add to the bowl

Liberally season with salt & pepper

Add in turmeric and olive oil and mix together

If it doesn't appear dark enough add in more turmeric

Put on a parchment lined baking sheet and bake for 30 minutes

Mains

Low Carb Keto Pasta

Yields 8 servings: Macros per serving: 4 net carb | 4.6g fat | 19g protein | 143 cal   [4/17 Video]

Ingredients:

2 cps King Arthur Keto flour 🛒

3 medium eggs

½ tsp kosher salt

½ Tbsp olive oil

Directions:

Thoroughly clean your work surface

Pour your flour into a heap on your work surface and mix in salt

Create a little well and crack in your eggs

Add olive oil

Knead all ingredients together with your hands

This flour is a little tougher than regular flour, keep kneading it and it will come together

Cut into 4 sections to make it easier to work with

Using a pasta machine, start on the thickest setting and run it through each setting 3 times until you get down to setting 1

Then cut it to your desired shape

If you cook it from fresh, only boil for 1 minute

If you let it dry out, boil it for 2 minutes

Cherry Tomato Feta Cheese Trend

Yields: 4 servings (w/ 1 lb chicken)   Macros per serving: 4.2g net carb | 30g fat | 43g protein | 475 cal   [2/2 Video]

Ingredients:

Cherry tomatoes   Salt & Pepper

Block of feta cheese   Olive Oil

1 bulb garlic   Red pepper flakes to taste (optional)

2-3 Tbsp basil

1-2 lbs boneless skinless chicken thighs

Directions:

Preheat oven to 400 °F

Put cherry tomatoes in glass baking dish with block of feta

Cut of the end of garlic bulb and put in glass dish

Add boneless skinless chicken thighs

Season everything with salt & pepper and add red paper flakes if you wish

Drizzle with olive oil

Bake for 40-45 minutes

Carefully squeeze the garlic cloves out of the garlic bulb, mix everything together and add fresh chopped basil

Camaron Yucatan

Yields: 1 servings   Macros per serving: 7 net carb | 1g fat | 12g protein | 90 cal   [1/31 Video]

Ingredients:

½ cp chopped romaine   2 cps cauli rice   squeeze lime juice

½ tomato   ½ small zucchini   salt & pepper to taste

½ small onion   ½ red bell pepper   cilantro (optional)

2 cloves garlic   5- 16/20 shrimp

Directions:

Put chopped romaine on a plate and set aside

To a food processor or high-power blender add onion, tomato and garlic and get it pureed

To a dry skillet add cauli rice and sweat out all of the moisture

Once it starts to turn brown add tomato puree

Chop the zucchini and red bell pepper and add to skillet

Cook through and put it all on the plate and set aside

To the skillet add the shrimp and a squeeze of lime juice

Cook through then put on top of cauli rice

This makes 1 serving, double or triple recipe as needed

Tri-Tip

Yields: 8 servings (depending on size)   Macros per serving: 1.3 net carb | 7.6g fat | 38g protein | 231 cal   [3/23 Video]

Ingredients:

Tri-Tip steak

Marinade:

¼ cp fresh lemon juice (reserve lemons for bag)

⅓ cp liquid aminos

½ cp olive oil

⅓ cp Worcestershire sauce

3 cloves minced garlic

1 Tbsp brown sugar swerve 🛒

½ tsp kosher salt

1 tsp pepper

½ tsp onion powder

2 tsp chilli lime (optional)

Directions:

Combine all marinade ingredients in a large ziplock bag then add your tri-tip

Let marinate for at least 24 hrs

Cook at 275 ºF until internal temperature reaches 128-132ºF

When done, put in hot oil in a cast iron skillet and reverse sear it

Let the meat rest 10-15minutes before slicing against the grain

Philly Cabbage Cheesesteak

Macros per cabbage steak: 5 net carb | 25g fat | 32g protein | 382 cal   [2/11 Video]

Ingredients:

1 small cabbage	1 package mushrooms	mushroom powder (optional)
2 tsp avocado oil	1 small onion	
1 pound steak cut thin	salt & pepper	

Directions:

Preheat oven to 400 ºF

Cut cabbage into cabbage steaks

Brush each cabbage steak with avocado oil, season with salt and pepper then bake for 30 minutes

While cabbage is cooking wash mushrooms and cut up onion

Season onion with salt, pepper and mushroom powder

Cook onion in a little oil in non-stick skillet

Once translucent add mushrooms and cook those down

Take onions and mushrooms out of the pan and set aside

Slice steak nice and thin

Put steak in the same skillet and heat until cooked all the way though

Grate some fresh sharp provolone

Put steak on top of cooked cabbage, top with onions and mushrooms

Grate some sharp provolone and sprinkle on top and put it back in oven until melty

Buffalo Chicken Bombs

Macros per bomb: 2.7 net carb | 13g fat | 12g protein | 186 cal

[3/4 Video]

Ingredients:

1 ½ cp mozzarella

2oz cream cheese

1 egg

1 ¼ cp almond flour 🛒

1 Tbsp baking powder

1 Tbsp oat fiber 🛒

1 large boneless skinless chicken breast cooked, shredded

salt & pepper to taste

hot sauce

egg wash

Directions:

Preheat oven to 350 ºF

First make your fathead dough by melting the mozzarella cheese and cream cheese in the microwave

Add to food processor with a dough blade

Drop in egg and mix it together

Now add in almond flour, baking powder and oat fiber

Wrap dough in cling wrap and put in freezer

Take shredded cooked chicken and mix in buffalo sauce and cream cheese

Take dough out of freezer and portion into 12 equal size balls

Flatten the dough ball, put some of the chicken mixture in the middle and wrap the dough around it to completely encase it

Brush with an egg wash and bake for 20-25 minutes

Optional: Serve with homemade blue cheese dressing (recipe)

Portobello Tacos

Yields: 6 servings   Macros per serving: 3 net carb | 17g fat | 16g protein | 287 cal

[3/7 Video]

Ingredients:

Ground beef

Taco Tuesday Seasoning-Flavor God 🛒

Portobello mushroom caps (or red bell peppers)

Pico de Gallo (recipe)

Sour cream

Cheddar

Directions:

Preheat oven to 375 ºF

Brown up ground beef and add Taco Tuesday seasoning

Wash mushroom caps and hollow out the inside (or cut red bell pepper in half and remove the seeds)

Stuff seasoned beef into mushroom caps and/or red bell pepper halves

Top with cheddar cheese and bake until cheese is melted

Top with fresh pico de gallo and sour cream

Buffalo Chicken Pizza

Yields: 8 slices   Macros per slice: 1.8 net carb | 15g fat | 21g protein | 231 cal   [3/27 Video]

Ingredients:

Crust:

1lb ground chicken

½ cp grated parmesan

1 egg

2 tsp Italian seasoning

½ tsp kosher salt

pepper to taste

½ tsp onion powder

Toppings:

Buffalo sauce

mozzarella cheese

red onion, sliced thin

ranch (recipe)

Directions:

Preheat oven to 400 °F

Mix all of the crust ingredients in a large bowl with your hands

Drop mixture onto parchment lined round pizza tray

Spread evenly all the way around the size of the whole pizza tray

Bake for 20 minutes until the edges are nice and browned

Add toppings

Pop back in oven until nice and toasty

Top with homemade ranch

Margherita Spaghetti Squash

Yields: 4 servings   Macros per serving: 5.4 net carb | 10g fat | 5g protein | 145 cal   [3/3 Video]

Ingredients:

1 spaghetti squash

1 Tbsp olive oil

Salt & pepper

Filling:

2 Tbsp olive oil

1 cp cherry tomatoes (chopped in half)

kosher salt

pepper   minced garlic

3 Tbsp fresh chopped basil

fresh mozzarella

Directions:

Preheat oven to 400 ºF

Cut spaghetti squash in half and remove all of the seeds

Brush with olive oil and season with salt and pepper

Bake flesh side down on a parchment lined baking sheet for 45 minutes

Scrape out the squash into a bowl and set aside and set the squash shells aside

Grab a non-stick skillet and add olive oil and the halved cherry tomatoes and cook with some kosher salt

Add fresh basil, pepper and minced garlic then add the squash back to the pan and give it a good mix

Stuff everything back into the shells of the squash

Top with basil and more mozzarella

Put back in oven until melted

Chicken Cordon Bleu Unwich

Macros per serving: 3 net carb | 27g fat | 37g protein | 417 cal

[3/17 Video]

Ingredients:

1 lb boneless skinless chicken breast

Salt & pepper

6 slices deli ham

Gruyere cheese

½ cp oat fiber 🛒

2 eggs

1 cp keto flour 🛒

1/2cp nutritional yeast 🛒

avocado oil

Directions:

Pat chicken dry and let come to room temp

Slice in half without going all the way through (butterfly)

Season with salt and pepper

Put 2 slices of ham on one side and top with gruyere cheese (or cheese of choice)

Secure closed with toothpicks

In one bowl add oat fiber

In a separate bowl beat 2 eggs

In a third bowl mix together keto flour and nutritional yeast

Dredge each one in oat fiber, then the egg, then the flour mixture

Fry in avocado oil until internal temperature reaches 165°F

Turkey Burger

Yields: 4 servings   Macros per serving: 1.5 net carb | 6g fat | 39g protein | 216 cal   [3/17 Insta]

Ingredients:

1 lb ground turkey

1 egg

1 Tbsp yellow mustard

2 tsp Worcestershire sauce

1/4 cup grated Parmesan

1/2 tsp chili powder

1/2 tsp Aleppo pepper (optional) 🛒

Kosher salt & pepper to taste

Directions:

In a large mixing bowl mix all ingredients together with hands and make 4 equal size patties
In a nonstick skillet add drizzle of olive oil.

Drop the patties in the hot pan and cover. Don't touch them for at least 3-4 min. Turkey burgers can fall apart easily if you mess with them.

Flip and then finish cooking through. Keep covered and add cheese until melted

Chorizo Stuffed Eggplant w/avocado cream sauce

Yields: 4 servings   Macros per serving: 6.5 net carb | 21g fat | 12g protein | 281 cal   [2-1 Insta]

Ingredients:

1 medium eggplant	4-5 links chorizo	
Salt & pepper	2 Tbsp fresh chopped parsley	
½ small white onion	½ tsp thyme	
2 Tbsp olive oil	1 tsp oregano	
2 cloves minced garlic	1 cp mozzarella	

Avocado Cream Sauce: (optional)

1 small ripe avocado

3 Tbsp water

3 Tbsp sour cream

pinch kosher salt

Directions:

Preheat oven to 400°F

Cut the top off of the eggplant and then cut in half lengthwise, leave about a half-inch border and scoop out the flesh

Liberally season eggplant with salt and pepper

Put in a parchment lined baking pan and set off to the side

Finely chop the eggplant flesh and white onion

Add the chopped eggplant and onion to a skillet with olive oil and cook for a couple minutes

Finely chop the chorizo (If the chorizo is in a casing remove it first)

Add the chorizo to the skillet and then add seasonings and cook it all the way through

Pat the eggplant boat dry with a paper towel and the stuff with the meat mixture and bake for 20 minutes

Take it out top with mozzarella an pop back in oven until cheese is melted

Top with avocado cream sauce (optional)

Honey Soy Glazed Porkchops

Macros per serving: 2.6 net carb | 8g fat | 45g protein | 312 cal

[3/16 Video]

Ingredients:

1 lb thick cut pork chops

¼ cp sugar free ketchup

3 Tbsp liquid aminos

3 Tbsp sugar free honey 🛒

2 cloves garlic minced

salt & pepper

Directions:

Allow porkchops to come up to room temp, then pat dry

Season with salt and pepper on all sides

Lightly grease indoor griddle or use a skillet

Sear porkchop on all sides

While porkchops are searing whisk the rest of the ingredients together in a small bowl

When the porkchops are about half-way done, brush with glaze

Continue cooking until porkchops reach an internal temperature of 145°F

Crockpot Salsa Verde Chicken

Yields: 8 servings   Macros per serving: 4.2 net carb | 9g fat | 22g protein | 203 cal   [3/14 Video]

Ingredients:

1/5 lb chicken breast or thighs

Salt & pepper

1 tsp cumin

1 tsp garlic powder

½ cp sour cream

1 cp Monterey jack

fresh cilantro

16oz jar salsa verde

Directions:

Season chicken all sides with salt, pepper, cumin and garlic powder

Put in a crockpot

Pour in salsa verde over top, cover and cook on low for 4hrs

Shred chicken and drain excess juice

Mix in sour cream and top with cheese of choice and top with fresh chopped cilantro

Put lid back on until the cheese melts

Eat on its own or wrap in some cabbage, lettuce or low carb tortilla

Pico Chicken Bake

Yields: 4 servings   Macros per serving: 4.2 net carb | 14g fat | 44g protein | 318 cal   [3/11 Video]

Ingredients:

Boneless skinless chicken breast

1 tsp garlic powder

1 tsp smoked paprika

1 tsp cumin

1 tsp black pepper

1 tsp kosher salt

2 cps fresh pico (recipe)

1 cp Monterey jack

cilantro

sour cream (optional)

Directions:

Preheat oven to 375 ºF

Allow chicken to come to room temperature (about 30 minutes)

Pat dry with a paper towel

Mix together all of the spices and rub all over the chicken on all sides

Put chicken in a casserole dish

Drain excess liquid from the pico and pour over top the chicken

Top with cheese of choice

Bake for 3o minutes or until chicken reaches 165ºF

Top with fresh cilantro and sour cream (optional)

Meatball Sub Cup

Macros per cup: 2.8 net carb | 16g fat | 17g protein | 229 cal

[3/8 Video]

Ingredients:

Fathead dough (recipe from buffalo chicken bombs)

Low carb sauce

Meatball (recipe) or frozen

mozzarella cheese

Italian zest-Flavor God 🛒

Directions:

Preheat oven to 375 ºF

Roll fat head dough into 12 equal size balls

Spray down muffin tin with non-stick spray

Press fathead dough into the bottom of each section

Put some past sauce in each one and add a meatball to each one

Top with mozzarella and sprinkle on some Italian Zest seasoning (or whatever seasoning you like)

Bake for 15-20 minutes until golden brown

Let sit for 5 minutes before taking out of muffin tin

Pan-seared Salmon

Macros per 3oz serving: 0 net carb | 24g fat | 19g protein | 296 cal

[2/5 Video]

Ingredients:

Filet of salmon-skin on

Kosher salt

pepper

Directions:

Pat salmon dry with paper towel

Liberally season with kosher salt and pepper on both sides

Heat up avocado oil or olive oil in a non-stick skillet

When it starts to shimmer lay fish skin side down and press down with fingers for just a second

(this will help get the sear and prevent the skin from rolling up)

Leave it untouched for 4 minutes and then flip and cook for another 4-5 minutes (depending on thickness)

Chicken Pad Thai

Yields: 5 servings   Macros per serving: 4.8 net carb | 10g fat | 20g protein | 192 cal   [2/3 Video]

Ingredients:

2 boneless skinless chicken breasts	1 jalapeno pepper
1 tsp chili sauce	1 tsp grated fresh ginger
3 tsp liquid aminos	½ large carrot ribboned
2 cps thinly sliced cabbage	2 Tbsp liquid aminos
1 cp thinly sliced red cabbage	1 green onion

Peanut Sauce:

1 Tbsp sesame oil	3 Tbsp natural PB
½ tsp turmeric	3 Tbsp liquid aminos
1 Tbsp avocado oil	½ tsp garlic chili sauce
2 Tbsp chopped peanuts	2 Tbsp lime juice
2 Tbsp fresh chopped cilantro	1 Tbsp Allulose

Directions:

Cube the chicken and cook thoroughly in a skillet with a little bit of olive oil

Add chili sauce and liquid aminos

Toss to coat and set aside

Add all ingredients for the peanut sauce to a small bowl and whisk together really well and set aside

Slice red cabbage and green cabbage really thin

Dice the jalapeno, grate the ginger, and peel the carrot

Using a peeler, keep peeling the carrot to create ribbons

To the same skillet you cooked the chicken in, add oil and prepared veggies, liquid aminos, green onion, sesame oil and turmeric

Once the mixture starts to wilt down a little bit add the peanut sauce

When the peanut sauce melts add the chicken back to the pan

Heat it through and then plate it and add some chopped peanuts to the top along with fresh cilantro

Roast Chicken

Macros per 3 oz serving: 0 net carb | 6g fat | 24g protein | 161 cal

[1/7 Video]

Ingredients:

1 whole chicken	4 cloves minced garlic
1 lemon	4 sprigs of rosemary
4 Tbsp butter	salt & pepper

Directions:

Preheat oven to 450ºF

Take bag out of cavity of chicken and clean the chicken by patting it completely dry inside and out

Liberally season the chicken inside and out with salt and pepper

Place chicken in a cast iron chicken

Cut lemon in half and stuff inside the cavity

In a small saucepan melt the butter with the minced garlic and brush over the entire chicken

Stuff some rosemary into the cavity with the lemon

Roast for 60 minutes to 1hr 15 minutes or until the internal temperature reaches 165ºF (I used a 4 pound bird)

Pork Roast

Macros per 3 oz serving: .2 net carb | 10g fat | 24g protein | 199 cal   [1/27 Video]

Ingredients:

Pork loin bone-in roast (this recipe is using a 5lb roast)

2 Tbsp avocado oil

2 Tbsp dijon mustard

2 tsp rosemary

1 tsp kosher salt

Pepper to taste

Directions:

Preheat oven to 450°F

Allow roast to come to room temperature and pat dry with a paper towel

Using a really sharp knife carefully score the top where the fat is, about ½ inch down in a crisscross pattern

Break apart a roasted garlic bouillon cube (or used minced garlic) and stuff into the scores of the roast

Mix remaining ingredients in a small bowl and brush the entire roast with it

Roast for 30 minutes

Without opening the oven door lower the heat to 350°F

Roast for another additional 55 minutes to 1 hour or until internal temperature reaches 155°F

Lemon Pepper Chicken Thighs

Yields: 4 servings   Macros per 2 thighs: 1.2 net carb | 43g fat | 64g protein | 333 cal   [1/28 Video]

Ingredients:

2 lbs skin on/bone in chicken thighs

4 Tbsp olive oil

4 Tbsp fresh lemon juice

Zest of 1 lemon

3 cloves minced garlic

2 tsp dry thyme

2 Tbsp brown sugar swerve 🛒

1 tsp onion powder

1 tsp kosher salt

Fresh cracked black pepper to taste

Directions:

Preheat oven to 400 ºF

To a large mixing bowl and all ingredients except for chicken

Using kitchen shears get rid of all of the excess fat on the chicken

Add chicken thighs to the bowl and toss to coat

Either let marinate for a couple hours or put right in the oven

Put chicken skin side up in a parchment line baking pan

Roast for 45 minutes

Throw under for 2 minutes to crisp up the skin

Squeeze fresh lemon juice over the top before serving

Chicken Thighs in a Thai coconut curry broth

Yields: 6 servings   Macros per serving: 3.8 net carb | 13g fat | 21g protein | 241 cal   [2/16 Video]

Ingredients:

2 lbs chicken thighs	1 large carrot	1 tsp fish sauce	2 cps fresh spinach
Salt & pepper	1 Tbsp fresh ginger	1 bay leaf	
1 Tbsp coconut water	2 cloves minced garlic	1 12 oz can coconut milk	
1 small white oniun	2 Tbsp red curry paste	1 cp low sodium chicken broth	

Directions:

Preheat oven to 400 ºF

Pat chicken thighs dry and season with salt and pepper

In the bottom of a double broiler or large stock pot heat up coconut oil and sear chicken on both sides 5 minutes

Remove and set aside

Chop up the onion and carrot and add to the same pan

When onions are translucent add ginger and garlic

Mix in the curry paste

Add the bay leaf, fish sauce, coconut milk and chicken broth

Mix together and add chicken back to the pot

Cover it and cook for an additional 15 minutes, then add fresh spinach

Cook until spinach wilts down

French Onion Chicken Bake

Yields: 4 servings   Macros per piece: 6.5 net carb | 19g fat | 44g protein | 393 cal   [1/13 Video]

Ingredients:

2 Tbsp butter

3 onions sliced thin

4 boneless skinless chicken breasts

Salt & pepper

1 Tbsp fresh chopped sage

1 Tbsp garlic paste

⅓ cp low sodium beef broth

1 cp shredded Gruyere cheese

Directions:

Preheat oven to 375ºF

Slice onions really thin and put into a nonstick skillet with butter

Cook for 15 minutes until caramelized

Add beef broth and garlic paste

Cook until liquid evaporates, put into a bowl and set aside to cool

Take chicken breast and slice in half lengthwise, not cutting all the way through (butterflying)

Season with salt, pepper and fresh sage

Shred fresh gruyere cheese

Add cheese and onion to one side of each chicken

Fold other side of chicken back over and secure with baking twine or toothpicks

Using the same pan from earlier, sear chicken on all sides

Put chicken in a casserole dish

Top with more onion and gruyere cheese

Bake for 25 minutes

Honey Lime Chicken Thighs

Yields: 8 servings   Macros per serving: 1 net carb | 6g fat | 31g protein | 224 cal

[1-14 Insta]

Ingredients:

2 lbs boneless skinless chicken thighs

1/4 cup sugar free honey 🛒

2 Tbsp liquid aminos

3 cloves minced garlic

1/2 tsp kosher salt

1/2 tsp kosher salt

3 Tbsp fresh lime juice

Zest of 1 lime

1-2 Tbsp Sriracha (optional)

2 Tbsp avocado oil

Directions:

Place thighs in airtight container and add all ingredients

Marinate for at least 2 hours up to overnight

Add avocado oil to skillet and sear on both sides until cooked through. About 5-6 min each side.

Meatball

Yields: 6 servings   Macros per serving: 2 net carb | 19g fat | 25g protein | 288 cal

[2-24 Insta]

Ingredients:

1 lb ground beef 85%

2 eggs

Salt & pepper to taste

2 cloves minced garlic

1/4 cup almond flour 🛒

1/4 cup dry grated Parmesan

1/4 cup fresh chopped parsley

1/2 cup fresh grated parmigiano-reggiano

Olive oil for drizzle

Directions:

Preheat oven to 350°F

Mix everything together except olive oil. Be careful to not over mix.

Roll into meatballs and place in baking dish.

Drizzle with olive oil and bake for 40 minutes, then add to sauce! (recipe)

Chicken Power Bowl

Yields: 2 bowls   Macros per bowl: 7 net carb | 34g fat | 41g protein | 515 cal   [2/18 Video]

Ingredients:

2 cps prepared cauli rice

2 boneless chicken breasts

Salt & pepper

Everything Spicy-Flavor God 🛒

3 Tbsp avocado oil

1 Tbsp butter

1 small yellow squash

½ cp cherry tomatoes

½ red pepper

1 cp fresh broccoli

2 Tbsp black garlic (or regular)

1 jalapeno pepper

1 avocado, sliced

Directions:

Allow chicken to come up to room temperature

Pat dry and season with salt and pepper and whatever seasoning you want. I used Everything Spicy from Flavor God

Get a skillet really hot and then add oil

Lay the chicken in away from you and don't touch for 4 minutes

Flip and cook through to 165ºF

Remove from pan

Add butter and veggies to the same pan

Cook through

Put veggies and chicken on top of cauli rice and top with avocado and homemade feta vinaigrette (recipe)

Turkey Stir-Fry

Yields: 6 servings   Macros per serving: 4.8 net carb | 19g fat | 22g protein | 274 cal   [2/26 Video]

Ingredients:

2-3 Tbsp olive oil	1 red pepper	1 egg	2 tsp fish sauce
1 lb ground turkey	1 yellow pepper	1 Tbsp fresh ginger	2 green onions
1 red chili pepper	1 cp mushrooms	2cloves garlic	
1 bag cauli rice	Bokchoy	¼ cp liquid aminos	

Directions:

Get a nonstick skillet nice and hot and then add oil

Add in the ground turkey

Chop red chili pepper and remove the seeds

Throw on top of the ground turkey

Grate the ginger and garlic over the top

Let meat sit there for a bit so it can caramelize. Once it starts to caramelize mix together

Once cooked, take out of the pan and set aside

Add some more oil to the pan and add red and yellow peppers, cook those through

Take your Bokchoy and remove leaves from the stems and chop everything up keeping leaves and stems separate

Add fish sauce and liquid aminos to peppers

Add Bokchoy stems and mushrooms, once cooked through add the leaves

Remove from pan and set aside

In the same pan cook an egg

Add cauli rice

Then add everything else back to the pan and mix

Treats

McGriddle in a Mug

Yields: 1 serving   Macros per serving: 3 net carb | 19g fat | 14g protein | 246 cal   [3/1 Video]

Ingredients:

2 Tbsp keto pancake mix 🛒

2 Tbsp water

1 Tbsp sugar-free maple syrup

1 egg scrambled

1 sausage patty

1 Tbsp cheddar

Directions:

Spray ramekin with cooking spray

Put some pre-made keto pancake mix at the bottom

Cook for 30 seconds, then top with sugar free maple syrup

Pour in scrambled egg, sausage and cheese and microwave for 1 minute

Thin Mint Mug Cake

Yields: 1 serving   Macros per serving: 5 net carb | 37g fat | 13g protein | 404 cal   [3/15 Video]

Ingredients:

1 Tbsp unsalted butter

3 Tbsp almond flour 🛒

2 Tbsp erythritol 🛒

1 Tbsp coco powder

½ tsp baking powder

pinch salt

½ tsp vanilla

¼ tsp mint extract

Filling:

2 Tbsp cream cheese

2 tsp powdered swerve 🛒

2-3 drops mint extract

Green food coloring (optional)

Directions:

In a microwave safe dish or mug melt butter

Add the rest of your cake ingredients and whisk together really well

Microwave on high for 90 seconds

Take out of dish or mug, cut in half and let it cool completely

In a separate bowl mix together filling ingredients until well combined

When the cake is cool put the filling mixture on one side and put the top of the cake back on

Chocolate Salted Caramel Lava Mug Cake

Yields: 1 serving   Macros per serving: 4 net carb | 30g fat | 11g protein | 330 cal   [3/8 Video]

Ingredients:

1 Tbsp unsalted butter

3 Tbsp almond flour 🛒

2 Tbsp erythritol 🛒

1 Tbsp coco powder

1 egg

pinch salt

½ baking powder

¼ tsp vanilla extract

8 squares salted caramel Lilly's bar

Directions:

In a microwave safe dish or mug melt butter

Add the rest of your cake ingredients (except for chocolate bar) and mix together really well

Once mixed stuff chocolate squares into the batter making sure its completely covered

Microwave on high for 60 seconds

Boston Cream Mug Cake

Yields: 1 serving   Macros per serving: 4.8 net carb | 52g fat | 11g protein | 529 cal   [2/15 Video]

Ingredients:

Pastry:

¼ cp heavy cream   1 Tbsp butter

1 egg yolk   ½ tsp vanilla extract

2 Tbsp powdered erythritol 🛒

1/8 tsp xanthan gum (if needed) 🛒

Cake:

1 Tbsp butter   ½ tsp vanilla extract

3 Tbsp almond flour   ½ tsp baking powder

2 Tbsp vanilla whey protein powder 🛒 1 egg

  2 Tbsp erythritol 🛒   2 Tbsp Lilys chips

Directions:

Add heavy cream to a saucepan- put heat on medium

In a separate bowl add egg yolk and sweetener and whisk together really well

Add butter and vanilla to heavy cream

Just before it comes to a boil take off the heat and slowly stream in egg yolk mixture

Sprinkle in some xanthan gum and whisk until thick, put in fridge to cool while you make your cake

In a microwave safe dish or mug melt butter

Add the rest of your cake ingredients and whisk together really well

Microwave on high for 90 seconds and then take out of dish or mug and let it cool completely

Once cool slice in half and add pastry cream to one half

Put the top back on the cake and melt some Lily's chocolate chips and spread on the top

Red Velvet Mug Cake

Yields: 1 serving   Macros per serving: 4.6 net carb | 32g fat | 13g protein | 372 cal   [2/8 Video]

Ingredients:

3 Tbsp almond flour 🛒

1 ½ Tbsp coconut flour 🛒

2 Tbsp erythritol 🛒

1 tsp cocoa powder

1 egg

1 Tbsp unsalted butter

1 pinch salt

3 Tbsp unsweetened almond milk

Directions:

In a microwave safe dish or mug melt butter

Add the rest of your cake ingredients and mix together really well

Microwave on high for 90 seconds

Top with sugar free whipped cream if desired

Nutella Mug Cake

Yields: 1 serving   Macros per serving: 5 net carb | 28g fat | 11g protein | 328 cal   [2/1 Video]

Ingredients:

1 Tbsp unsalted butter   1 egg

3 Tbsp keto flour (or almond flour) 🛒   1 tsp baking powder

2 Tbsp erythritol 🛒   pinch salt

½ Tbsp pyure hazelnut spread 🛒

Directions:

In a microwave safe dish or mug melt butter

Add the rest of your cake ingredients and whisk together really well

Microwave on high for 90 seconds

While cake is cooling, melt a tiny bit more of the hazelnut spread in the microwave and then drizzle on top of the cake

Strawberry Shortcake Mug Cake

Yields: 1 serving   Macros per serving: 5 net carb | 24g fat | 15g protein | 305 cal   [1/18 Video]

Ingredients:

Whipped cream: Cake:

1/8 cp heavy cream   1 Tbsp unsalted butter   1 egg   ½ tsp baking powder

¼ tsp vanilla extract   5 Tbsp almond flour 🛒   pinch salt   2 whole strawberries sliced

½ tsp powdered erythritol 🛒   2 Tbsp erythritol 🛒   ½ tsp vanilla

Directions:

Put all of your whipped cream ingredients in a bowl and mix together using a handmixer

Whip until thick and put in fridge while you make your cake

In a microwave safe dish or mug melt butter

Add the rest of your cake ingredients and mix together really well

Microwave on high for 90 seconds

Take out of mug or dish to cool

Once cooled slice in half and sprinkle erythritol on each side

Put a dollop of homemade whipped cream on one side

Slice 1 strawberry and put pieces on top of the whipped cream

Put the top back on the cake and finish with another dollop of whipped cream and another sliced strawberry

Gingerbread Cream Mug Cake

Yields: 1 serving   Macros per serving: 4 net carb | 30g fat | 10g protein | 335 cal   [1/4 Video]

Ingredients:

Cake:

1 Tbsp butter

3 Tbsp keto flour 🛒

2 Tbsp erythritol 🛒

1 egg

¼ tsp baking powder

½ tsp gingerbread extract 🛒

2 tsp Flavor God Gingerbread Seasoning 🛒

Frosting:

1 oz room temp cream cheese

1 Tbsp powdered erythritol 🛒

¼ tsp vanilla extract

Directions:

Put butter in a microwave safe dish or mug and microwave for 2 minutes until browned

Add the rest of the cake ingredients and whisk together until well combined

Microwave on high for 90 seconds and set aside to cool

In a separate bowl cream together all frosting ingredients

Once the cake is cool, frost the top and sprinkle more gingerbread seasoning on the top

Chocolate Peanut Butter Mug Cake

Yields: 1 serving   Macros per serving: 5 net carb | 37g fat | 16g protein | 415 cal   [1/11 Video]

Ingredients:

1 Tbsp unsalted butter

5 Tbsp almond flour 🛒

1 Tbsp unsweetened cocoa powder

1 ½ Tbsp erythritol 🛒

pinch salt

1 egg

½ tsp vanilla extract

1 tsp natural peanut butter

Lily's chips for topping (optional)

Directions:

Melt butter in a microwave safe bowl or mug

Add the rest of your ingredients (except for peanut butter) and whisk together until well combined

Drop dollops of peanut butter on top

Using a tooth pick swirl the peanut butter through the batter

Microwave on high for 90 seconds

Optional: Add Lily's chips to the top and allow to melt

Pineapple Upside Down Mug Cake

Yields: 1 serving   Macros per serving: 4 net carb | 23g fat | 14g protein | 279 cal   [2/22 Video]

Ingredients:

1 Tbsp butter

1 Tbsp brown sugar swerve 🛒

1 Tbsp pineapple chunks

1 Tbsp vanilla whey protein powder 🛒

3 Tbsp almond flour 🛒

½ tsp baking powder

1 egg

2 Tbsp erythritol 🛒

½ tsp vanilla

¼ tsp pineapple extract 🛒

1 Tbsp almond milk

Directions:

Add butter, brown sugar and pineapple chunks to a microwave safe bowl

Melt butter and set aside

In a separate bowl add all of the remaining ingredients and mix really well

Pour on top of pineapple mixture and then microwave on high for 90 seconds

Strawberry Frozen Yogurt

Macrus per ¼ cp: 4.4 net carb | 1.6 g fat | 2.7g protein | 46 cal

(3/29 Video)

Ingredients:

1 cup plain Greek yogurt

2 cps frozen strawberries

3 Tbsp unsweetened almond milk

2-3 Tbsp confectioners swerve 🛒

1 tsp vanilla extract

Directions:

Add all ingredients to a high-power blender

Blend on high for 2-3 minutes until creamy

Pour into a container and put in freezer for at least 1 hr

Take out of freezer 10 minutes before enjoying

Cheesecake for 2

Yields: 2 servings   Macros per serving: 5 net carb | 42g fat | 12g protein | 480 cal   [1/25 Video]

Ingredients:

Crust:

7 Tbsp almond flour 🛒

2 Tbsp unsalted butter

2 Tbsp erythritol 🛒

½ tsp graham cracker extract 🛒

Filling:

5oz room temp cream cheese   1 tsp lemon zest

2 Tbsp powdered erythritol 🛒   1 tsp fresh lemon juice

1 egg

½ tsp vanilla extract

Directions:

Melt butter and then add rest of your crust ingredients

Press crust into the bottom of 6 oz ramekins or even a coffee mug

In another bowl add filling ingredients and whisk together until smooth

Pour on top of crusts

Microwave 1 at a time for 1 minute each

Put in fridge for 1 hr to set before enjoying

**Optional-Top with blueberries before serving

Blueberry Lemon Scones

Yields: 8 servings   Macros per serving: 4.7 net carb | 16g fat | 6.8g protein | 205 cal   [3/13 Video]

Ingredients:

2 cps keto flour 🛒

½ cp erythritol 🛒

½ tsp salt

1 tsp baking powder

1 egg

⅓ cp unsweetened almond milk

1 tsp lemon extract 🛒

1 tsp vanilla extract

3 Tbsp unsalted butter-melted

¾ cp fresh blueberries

Directions:

Preheat oven to 350ºF

Add all dry ingredients to mixing bowl or stand mixer and mix together (except for melted butter)

In a separate bowl whisk together wet ingredients and then put into dry mixture then add melted butter

Mix together but be careful to not overmix.

Fold in blueberries by hand.

Drop onto parchment paper and press into a large circle that is completely even all the way across

Sprinkle top with erythritol and cut circle into triangles (like pie slices)

Separate triangles and bake for 25 – 30 minutes, until golden brown

Let sit out on counter for 10-15 minutes to firm up before enjoying.

Peanut Butter Protein Cookies

Yields: 22 cookies   Macros per cookie: .8 net carb | 5.8g fat | 6.6g protein | 82 cal   [2/23 Video]

Ingredients:

1 cp natural peanut butter   2 eggs

¾ cp erythritol 🛒   1 tsp vanilla

½ cp vanilla whey protein powder 🛒

Directions:

Preheat oven to 350 ⁰F

Add your natural peanut butter to a large mixing bowl along with the rest of the ingredients

Using a small cookie scoop (or roll out 1 inch balls by hand) drop cookies onto parchment lined baking sheet and smash down with a fork creating

Criss-cross

Bake for 10 minutes

*make sure peanut butter is just peanuts and maybe salt

Key Lime Pie Fat Bombs

Yields: 19 servings   Macros per serving: 1 net carb | 6.6g fat | 1.2g protein | 69 cal   (1/29 Video)

Ingredients:

Crust:

½ cp keto flour (or almond flour) 🛒

4 Tbsp unsalted butter
🛒

2 Tbsp powdered erythritol 🛒

1/2tsp vanilla

Filling:

6oz room temp cream cheese

3 Tbsp fresh lime juice

zest 1 lime

5 Tbsp unsweetened almond milk

1 tsp vanilla

⅓ cp powdered erythritol

Directions:

Melt butter in a microwave safe bowl and then add the rest of your curst ingredients and mix well

Press 1 tsp of crust mixture into each space of silicone mold (or use mini cupcake liners)

Add softened cream cheese to a bowl with the rest of the filling ingredients

Using a hand mixer, whip until nice and smooth

Pour onto prepared crusts and put in freezer for 2 hours

Store in freezer and take out 15 minutes before enjoying

Silicone mold on Amazon 🛒

Cookies n Cream Fat Bombs

Yields: 24 servings   Macros per serving: 3.2 net carb | 5.7g fat | .8g protein | 68 cal   [1/22 Video]

Ingredients:

Cookie Crumbles:

¼ cp almond flour 🛒   pinch salt

1 room temp egg   2 Tbsp melted unsalted butter

¼ tsp baking powder   2 tsp heavy cream

¼ cp erythritol 🛒   ¼ tsp vanilla

1 ½ Tbsp unsweetened cocoa powder

White Chocolate:

2 Tbsp coconut oil

7oz Lily's white chips

Directions:

Preheat oven to 325 ºF

Add all dry cookie crumble ingredients to a mixing bowl and whisk together to get out all of the lumps

In another bowl whisk room temp egg white until frothy

Add the egg white, yolk and rest of the wet cookie crumble ingredients to the bowl and fold all ingredients together

Spread onto parchment line baking sheet as thin as you can get it

Bake for 20 minutes. Once cool, break it into crumbles and set aside.

Melt coconut oil and Lily's chips together in a microwave safe bowl

Mix in cookie crumble and pour mixture into silicone mold

Put in fridge until it solidifies

Cake Pop Fat Bombs

Yields: 18 cake pops   Macros per cake pop: 1.1 net carb | 8.5g fat | 2.1g protein | 90 cal   [1/15 Video]

Ingredients:

1 ½ cp almond flour 🛒

½ cp powdered erythritol 🛒

3 Tbsp room temp unsalted butter

2 oz room temp cream cheese

pinch salt

1 tsp vanilla extract

1 tsp cake batter extract 🛒

2 Tbsp SF sprinkles 🛒

Icing:

⅓ cp powdered erythritol 🛒

4 Tbsp heavy cream

½ tsp vanilla extract

Directions:

Add dry ingredients to a mixing bowl. Get out all big lumps with a whisk or fork

Add room temp butter, cream cheese and extract. Mix it all together with a fork until a dough forms.

Fold in sugar free rainbow sprinkles

Roll in to equal size balls

Mix icing ingredients together really well in a small bowl and dip each ball to coat all sides

Top with sugar free sprinkles

Keep in fridge in airtight container

Twix Fat Bombs

Yields: 24 servings   Macros per serving: 1.5 net carb | 9.2g fat | 1.7g protein | 97 cal   [1/1 Video]

Ingredients:

Cookie Layer:

4 Tbsp unsalted butter

1 ¼ cp almond flour 🛒

1 tsp vanilla extract

¼ tsp salt

Carmel Layer:

5 Tbsp unsalted butter

½ cp brown sugar swerve 🛒

¼ cp allulose 🛒

½ tsp vanilla

pinch sea salt

¼ tsp xanthan gum 🛒

½ cp heavy cream

Top Layer:

6 oz Lily's chips, melted

Directions:

Cookie layer:

In a small saucepan melt unsalted butter and then mix in the rest of the cookie layer ingredients. Mix until combined.

Using a teaspoon press equal an amount of mixture into each section of silicone mold

Caramel layer:

To a saucepan add the butter, brown sugar swerve and allulose

Melt on med-low until "sugar" dissolves

Take off heat and immediately add heavy cream and vanilla, whisk constantly

Put back on low heat and add salt and xanthan gum and whisk until very thick

Allow to cool about 10 minutes and add to cookie layer. Once cool, pour equal amount over each cookie layer and put in freezer to set for1 hr

Top layer:

In a microwave safe bowl melt Lily's chocolate

Pour over each section of silicone mold and let it set in the freezer before enjoying

*Store in airtight container in fridge   Silicone mold on Amazon 🛒

Glazed Cinnamon Donuts Fat Bombs

Yields 12 dount fat bombs: Macros per donut: : .5 net carb | 10g fat | 2.2g protein | 111 cal   [1/8 Video]

Ingredients:

Unrefined coconut oil	½ tsp ginger
¾ cp keto flour 🛒	½ tsp baking powder
1 tsp psyllium husk powder 🛒	1 tsp cake batter extract 🛒
1 tsp cinnamon	pinch kosher salt
3 Tbsp powdered erythritol 🛒	2 eggs
2 Tbsp unsalted butter, melted	

Glaze:

1 oz room temp cream cheese

⅓ cp powdered erythritol 🛒

4 Tbsp heavy cream

½ tsp cinnamon

Directions:

To a small saucepan add unrefined coconut oil. Add enough that when it is melted it completely submerges the donut holes

In a large mixing bowl add all of the dry ingredients

Now add your wet ingredients to the dry ingredients and mix with a hand mixer and beat until combined and a bit sticky

Let sit for 3 minutes so the psyllium husk can do its job

Roll out into equal size balls

Heat the coconut oil to 330°F

Carefully drop in a few donut holes at a time

They will flip themselves over when they are ready to flip

Take out and put on paper towel to drain

Cream together all of your glaze ingredients

Dip each donut hole in the glaze

Made in the USA
Columbia, SC
12 November 2021